Sneaking

THROUGH THE

Evening

Sneaking
THROUGH THE
Evening

NEW POEMS BY
MAUREEN McCARTHY

HARBOUR PUBLISHING

For my children, John and Anne

Published by
HARBOUR PUBLISHING
P.O. Box 219
Madeira Park, BC Canada
V0N 2H0

THE CANADA COUNCIL FOR THE ARTS SINCE 1957 | LE CONSEIL DES ARTS DU CANADA DEPUIS 1957

Cover photograph by Keith Thirkell
Printed and bound in Canada

Harbour Publishing acknowledges the financial support of the Government of Canada through the Book Publishing Industry Development Program (BPIDP) and the Canada Council for the Arts, and the Province of British Columbia through the British Columbia Arts Council, for its publishing activities.

"Shapelessness," "Blue Dreams," "Full of Time," "Bivouacs," and "Feet" have previously appeared in *Event*.

Canadian Cataloguing in Publication Data

McCarthy, Maureen, 1944–
   Sneaking through the evening

Poems.
ISBN 1-55017-216-6

I. Title.
PS8575.C419S63 1999   C811'.54   C99-910895-6
PR9199.3.M292S63 1999

Contents

SHAPELESSNESS

Rooms stretch into shapelessness,
stairs fall off in sudden drops,
walls are water marked by tides –
still, I hope to make my way
without leaving home,
set off from the parlour
at a pre-arranged time,
a ham sandwich folded in my pocket,
the past balanced on my head –
when I reach the doldrums
I'll warm up memories
cold in corners,
study Shakespeare,
then I'll sit down, put some soup on,
tomato, I suppose,
and wait for night to shine
with all its reds, yellows, blues,
oh those blues,
they remind me of satin dresses locked away,
where is the key, what is the melody?

THE STREETS

Wind races through the streets,
swoops up flowers with their heads cut off,
scurries up the hills to eat them –
who'll be next?
Grab onto a pole, anything to save yourself,
remember a twenty dollar bill is hidden
in the shoe
and a modest faith, broken by the seasons,
its eyes bandaged with magnolia.
When darkness falls, sneak off with your resumes,
your feather boas,
perhaps we'll pass each other running,
me with the whole East End of Montreal
stuffed in my ass pocket,
to keep me from forgetting
who I am.

POCKET

Who doesn't like to put into their pocket
the little nothing that they know –
the way they marched on winter
with their nails varnished green,
their placards painted over with ripe tomatoes –
the way they underlined a name
with three red lines,
a name round as Valentino –
the way their fresh starts all returned
to slush and darkening skies,
the last two blocks before home.
Who doesn't like to put into their pocket
the little nothing that they know
as they stand in line at cash machines
for ruinous money to throw at dreary days,
and all around is thunder, leaves and speckled birds,
rain, that endless, wild confusion.

THE RAGGED BODY

The ragged body is blown into that sea
of endless longing
that swirls around the house –
I sit in the bathroom window,
blow smoke rings down –
there's Aunty Pat with her Mae West hair, still afloat,
we wave,
I have just climbed out,
my thoughts are soaked,
their stems twisted,
but soon I will dive in again –
My course is long. I stretch my frame
from floor to roof,
fill my legs with pompoms,
my arms with Irish poetry –
I listen to the tides to slow my blood,
help it thicken,
watch the moon trail its joy across the vacant lot,
over the huge boulder
over snails, slugs, garter snakes –
I ask everyone directions to the house
where things get sorted out –
I'm putting on my lilac dress,
my French parfum,
I'm singing in advance. I'm thinking
that I'll get there.

Ambiguity has kept me squished in corners,
my eyes like stars crossing the blue expanse
of vague desire –
Knowingness eluded me, what was left
but hesitation,
and being caught at midnight
on lawns not my own
searching for peace, that hunted animal.
The sun buried his face in cloudy pillows,
crows hooted,
what was left
but mistakes and starting over,
but the lonely gaiety of butterflies
floating like a mist above the water.
I pray for slowness to surround me,
to rush around my feet.
I divide my body into sections,
one to deal with terror, one to deal with joy,
one to deal with darkness wandering the streets,
eating up the houses, snapping at my bones.

My Corner of the Clock

I'm crouching in my corner of the clock,
my throat a little raspy from those lies,
my dull handle on the world hidden in the rim
of a felt hat
and I'm thinking about thought –
how it drains me,
turns me white –
a crocus is growing from my hand,
what can I write down,
nothing, nothing,
but puffs of smoke
and a HO HO sound –
but soon I'll have the sofa to myself again,
I'll lie down,
roll my shoulders up around my ears,
think of Verdi and his Requiems,
think of father, with his lily hands,
his delphinium tie –
that row of crosses,
think of March winds, the stragglers,
and those who ran off
afraid that they would faint or vomit –
my throat made little mousey cries
as I turned into the street,
my face buried itself in the collar of my coat,
my mind tied itself to a tree
so it wouldn't lose itself,
now branches are growing through it,
dancing me around when breezes blow.

We were hauled by our hair
through the calendar –
the whole twelve months twirled us round,
our legs dangling like loose strings
in strong espresso weather.
Damp acres hiding under midnight called out
for sly animal feet.
Yes, you have to be a wily walker
as the anchors tattooed on your heart
haul you down –
you have to sit in back rooms,
behind draperies
where everything occurs –
your shadows near the light,
their noses pierced with the ruby O of love,
sit, sit still,
gawking at nothing, whistling.

TEETH

My teeth flare, all 10 of them,
the empty spaces like open doors
sucking in the drafty darkness,
listen to the downpour,
even the soul grows damp
wishes to be in Florida
swooning among orange groves –
to hell with winter
this compost heap of shames and terrors –
where is my prey?
I am hungry, hungry for ideas –
lightning shoots across the floor,
my moustache flies like wild grass into my yellow eyes
as I spring –
I can't stop, though I know
the good ones will escape
slither underneath the bed.
They'll whirl and fart around dust balls,
discarded New Yorkers, chipped cups, a hanger,
they'll shriek with laughter.
I'm staggering with my blankets
toward resignation,
toward the light inside the fridge.
I'm roaming through carrots,
slices of roast beef, a lemon meringue pie –
I'm gathering in my sanity again, my little hums and
    whistles.

FOR ROY

I sport a razor cut,
a military jacket,
ride the skytrain as if I were a general, off duty,
idly viewing wet sloppy streets,
the homeless,
dead places that used to be alive.
My thoughts blare,
people move away, turn their secret faces.
At which station should I get off
descend into capitalism?
I ride back and forth all day, waiting for a signal
from the CIA
and counting the umbrellas,
the opened versus the unopened.
The inspector is advancing, checking tickets –
I'll tell him about Socrates,
and that I'm used to being ejected –
to my limbs being pulled by ropes through hospital
    wards
and boarding houses,
under lakes, sealed with thick ice,
up through failure, loneliness and grief.

Everyone is busy, coming – going,
their eyes like searchlights
seeking glimpses –
cedars darken as night descends –
one swings back and forth, cooled by sparkling
    breezes,
by the pitch and roll of new ideas,
but then one wants to lie down,
not be bothered –
to sink deeper into the drowsy ditch,
watch people jump across above,
their briefcases jangling,
their feet dislodging stones that rumple down,
the ground shakes from the pounding,
candles are blown out, must be relighted
at tables covered with checkered tablecloths,
hands are ready with their knives and forks
the wine's abundant, a canary sings –
are you not happy now?

Be Off

I must be off and be away
and yet I circle round and round
against my will and ravenous –
will there be directives from the tower?
Hints hidden from the frivolous, the hurried?
My eyes rush out like lunatics before me,
what can I do to still them,
what can I do?
I pray for friends to save me
to keep me from the news,
to act in my name,
because I'm stuck here on Jarry Street
examining the dust, the three yellow tulips,
the iron railing leading up the six front stairs,
the evening light,
things that can never be explained.

A Hiss

A hiss snakes around pretty prayers
and across the inky quiet,
falls onto perfume bottles, the little statue
of the Blessed Virgin.
It chewed up Monday, was absent Tuesday,
what is its name,
this traveller with the long nose poking
into sugar bowls?
Will it be I who corners him,
picks him up by his prickly tail,
carries him up the winding stairs
as if he was a friend, exhausted?
Will it be I you'll see
sitting by the kitchen window,
among spoons and teacups,
waving into the nothingness?
Will it be I who lies beneath the cherry tree,
reading,
in a summer that's grown old, but still is warm?

UNEASE

Unease with all her clickers clacking
burrows into the brain,
wakes me from my coma –
what are those fumes?
What is that scraping sound – a branch against the
    house?
rain streams down the window panes –
the room is still, hidden away,
a box within a box within a box,
a lantern lamp evades –
who will lead me out
into the kitchen,
yes, it's often thought to be unreachable –
but let's put our heads together,
plot a course,
gather horses, provisions, swords –
but what you ask, you lazy good for nothing,
about the twists and turns,
the burials,
and who will be in charge?

SPEED

I like to pick up speed
as I fly through melancholy hours,
a trumpet in one hand,
my feet delicately arranged a little to the left
and treading air –
It's not easy –
for afternoon pulls me East,
night into the furies that lie West.
I search the fields below for armchairs,
specifically, for an overstuffed recliner –
one I can plop down in, swivel back,
study the clouds, their fluffy ways –
and they can study me,
see how my hands and wrists drift off the arm rests,
how my feet dangle in mid air,
how my body is broken into journeys,
my mind lost in odd wanderings.

I'm partial to rebellion
and warm rooms,
dusk stealing across the ceiling
soaking up the light,
while I sit scouring the classifieds –
I'm searching for a pilot, double qualified,
to pilot me through sea and air,
one who can cross borders clandestinely
when inspectors are asleep,
slumped inside their cages –
how many lipsticks should I bring,
how many bold canaries?
but who can answer for another?
The plane glistens on the runway,
silver in the frothy moonlight,
and I am in a bus racing toward it –
mother cheers me on,
and all the faces I have loved
smile in the window –
hydrangeas bloom in empty seats,
stops fly by, and winter passes.

One Day

One day I stayed in
and never left again –
now I inch around in a zigzag suit between epics,
rooms crammed with nostalgia,
eat bacon and eggs,
am unquestioning,
but full of questions.
Wind storms harangue my thoughts,
blow me about the 1950's
blow me against the sparseness of father's speech –
perhaps he was a ghost who chain smoked, after all.
Maps traced on the floor lead to reckonings.
Sometimes I go up to the attic
lie on the old beds,
listen to my favourite city humming in my chest,
wear myself out with drifting lamentations –
sometimes I carry my bike over mountainous furniture
and though floods,
speed against the light across the kitchen,
because I hear the postman
and am awaiting words of happiness and love.

The best thing on cold nights is bed –
you have to try it –
you can study your Michelin maps of Paris
and of Rome,
trace the Arno,
or listen to the radio,
it has every sort of accent, some as strong as onions,
you can stay up emptying drawers
in search of spring,
or pace around the outskirts of the little rug
and try to remember the year you became a
    miniaturist –
you can adopt a cry, fierce and grinding,
keep it in your handbag
for encounters with the mean spirited,
or change course and circle back
into the bathroom,
brush the thinning hair,
prepare for the wilderness that lies ahead

BEGIN AGAIN

I'll begin again with afternoon,
the bird with its feathers tilted up
scooting like a little emperor through his palace,
autumn going on.
I set out from autumn many times
but always have returned to that straw chair
in the back yard
from which I can trace nothing,
not the traffic of the leaves
or the silence that goes like a huge animal
through our thoughts –
should one be on guard against it
or try to deserve it?
It watches me
clutching my possessions to my breast,
and hoping no one will grab them off me,
hoping no one will try.

THE FUTURE WAITS

The future waits
but I am drifting westwards
past the smells of yesterday,
the gasoline ,the beer,
the garlic and salami,
the jasmine scent on crowded buses.
The March earth stinks
though the breeze is fresh,
and I am floating through a snow melt,
a woollen hat stuffed inside my pocket
for the first time in four months –
spring is wrapping round the spine,
perhaps it is inoperable
and will blossom between discs for years to come
though the mind loses confidence
and wanders off toward grief.

EATON'S

I'm going down to Eaton's
to buy a record of a train travelling,
a train slipping through the tunnels,
sparks shooting from its engine.
I'm going to jump aboard –
say goodbye,
kiss me slowly on my changing cheek,
or come along,
down the fire escape,
past grandma dozing in her chair,
past the school,
the teacher posting up exam scores,
past fathers fleeing failures,
their cries a block behind them,
dying in smouldering August air –
we'll take the greasy dog from the garage,
watch him smile at our genius,
one day we'll write a letter home,
say we were grateful for the start,
for our eventual place among the dead,
for the stars.

GRANDMA

Grandma, grandma,
come out of hiding –
sit here and we'll snort like horses
at these spindly trees,
these weeds and leaky pipes,
we'll hang about,
wait for the Second Coming,
add a few lines to the composition of our lives,
not be too untruthful –
the pale violet of the sky is stretching
around the corner –
we'll take a cab, follow it,
continue the long chase after beauty,
we'll not grow weary, grandma,
or am I wrong again?
Well then we'll rest grandma,
put our feet up against the bar of night,
eat a hamburger,
watch starlings build their nests,
what sturdy craftsmen,
should we ask them grandma
who their influences are?
Ask if we should wear white,
so the moon can spot us,
know where to shine his light?

CAUGHT

Caught in the flood of evening
we're drifting with our salvoes,
our fleshy legs hanging overboard,
gulls screaming,
as if their minds had all collapsed at once –
what floats beneath –
is it the dead tossing in their winter coats?
I shine my flashlight down
see the top of a submerged car,
a brown maroon,
or is it spilled reason,
or father's head
still filled with watery worlds
and Old Niagara Sherry?
A wind rises,
sweeps us under railroad bridges,
past deserted bird filled islands,
past the garden gate,
night is following –
who sent it?
Go back, go back, we holler,
or you will not be forgiven,
will not be forgiven.

DEO GRATIAS

Deo gratias
sing my sparrows, sing my toes,
as evening's velvet yellow trickles in
from winter's heartland –
I settle in night's groove,
forget about the old carry on,
with its windy ways, its pompadours,
its glossy belly sliding down into the sea –
ghosts lead me on a leather leash,
but an emerald moth flutters on my hand,
dreams with tiny muscles
arranged in herringbone design,
they whisper they will be the guide,
O snail my love, come comfort me.

NOWHERE

Nowhere, nowhere, dearest –
I am going nowhere
but into steamy baths,
wearing lacy lies, illusions –
I like to keep them on –
sometimes we sit together
moonlight on our forehead,
a cigarette dangling from pink lips,
the cat in our arms,
and think what a nice portrait
we make,
but we can't last forever.
I'm going to bed dearest,
am pulling up the blankets
and welcoming the hands that lift my body into sleep,
the sounds that come from nowhere.

LUCY

Lucy, you're a wreck abandoned
on this most abandoned stretch,
erratic movements scrawled across the dark
illuminate miles of empty wine bottles,
a sister, a piano –
Lucy, you need a bath,
a new set of dentures,
a pack of cigarettes –
your great grandma, on a pilgrimage
to St. Isadore's well, was caught by Goya,
the night was thick with black smoke,
the road muddy,
but the road will never be your friend,
for you head is woven with fatigue,
forgetfulness,
in your hand is a mirror of time vanishing,
words fading,
not even the image of a breeze remains.

BLUE DREAMS

Blue dreams flutter their grey wings –
tired, have they grown tired
of crashing into trees?
Explanations fold their pages and depart –
night draws the earth and sky together,
there is the swish of witches switching
North and South around –
the weather whirls,
its cheeks red as geraniums.
The doctor said to stay in bed
and read romances,
to eat tiny cups of Angel Gabriel light,
to keep my hands clean, clean, he said,
to forget everything,
the wars, the lies, the dead,
the way some died,
their arms flailing like ringing bells
heard in the hills
above the sheep's low heads.

FORESTS

Through the forests of the mind
she flits, a wasp
in her red dress, yellow gloves,
scowling –
all her thoughts are hot and lazy
and enmeshed,
her sins make a cheerful sound,
like crickets chirping –
she has a parasol that she can fling,
or beat the grass with,
give it a merry thrashing –
are there lion snakes in hiding?
The forest whispers to itself,
the way that forests do,
talks above her head –
her ears are twisted out,
still she fails to catch a meaning –
the plants are thick and strange and growing fast,
what a lonely sight she is –
no one, no one is near,
oh my dear!

FULL OF TIME

Full of time I knock around the house,
flip coins,
heads, I'm setting out –
tails, I'm lying on the couch,
surrendering –
humbly yours, and nothing to be done –
knowledge, knowledge,
I was a seeker after,
especially on hot nights
at work, alone,
with the very ill, their stillness
like a vague massive form, engulfing,
their breathing tapping at the door.
Who goes there?
no answer –
humbly yours,
the coin has been 10 years in the air –
leaves are falling
and November stumbles with his bag of rainy colours,
they spill onto cartops,
split along soft lines,
the tough, what do they know?
Full of time, I knock around the house.

I travel around sparrows washing
their wings in dirt –
around the back yard, knee deep
in water,
around that wild gardenia from Woolworth's
the aunts wore on Sunday afternoons
when they discussed horse races,
sipped gin,
I carry my own memories,
rest between hope and longing –
go over everything again,
how I took three scissor steps left, into the sea,
how grandma came with blintzes,
a priest,
a wool crepe jacket,
how they all slapped me on wet cheeks,
called me back.
I examine the wooden fence again –
rain lashes it, and then light arrives.
Squirrels run across the top –
September, October, the dogwood blooms –
I love those creamy blossoms,
I go right over to them –
I could never stay away.

TWITTERING

Birds are twittering,
is it for Mama?
Where is she,
why is she not answering?
Mama, mama,
perhaps she has been wounded
and is being transported on a stretcher
by bewildered crows –
Hold on mama, hold on,
don't be dismayed by grumpy carriers,
tight bandages,·
hold on –
in the desert is a bed
with a triangular lift
for hoisting up on,
with rococo side rails
and beside it a plush commode,
and though the sands of time
fall into the beak
and language breaks,
rolls into dirty corners,
is at the mercy of rats,
hold on mama,
chirp tomorrow's song.

In Bed

I lie in bed,
eat chocolates and smoke cigarettes,
look out at lights twinkling in the burbs,
trees, like fans, cooling down the houses.
Do you hear the heat rising,
rolling off the tables?
It lands inside the hollows of the night,
melts insomniacs
who drift about
examining the clothes in crowded cupboards,
waking up the birds –
wondering which July this is,
remembering father slipping into death,
an orange in one hand,
as if anyone could do it
if they wanted to.
Remembering the stillness
that leaked from the coffin
and filled people's mouths.
It was a stillness like a truth,
and how many truths, can you remember?

FOR ANNE

A ticking sound runs past the injured,
the undecided,
those with dripping noses,
the taverns and the old days,
buses at the loop,
past black balls, honey moons, jelly babies,
the woman behind the counter reading, "Allo Police",
I hear it in the silence of my ditch,
take an hypnotic,
snuggle in –
I like to plot my future when I rest,
I'm going to swim through March,
avoid the "Ides",
keep one eye on my rages, one eye on my dolours,
one eye on crows shrieking about starvation,
one eye on the stars, they're at loose ends,
aren't they wonderful? Like shepherds
I take them for a sign,
I'm going to sleep through March,
you'll know me by my snores,
I'll lift my head in April, on the eighth,
for you, my jelly baby.

HOAXES

Hoaxes roam the humming streets,
blinds descend,
sleepers wander through disjointed dreams,
some on horseback –
what is there to steal?
Tossed out sacs of prospects, losses,
satin wishes shredded –
a few could be fashioned into hats
with starry edges
and worn to meetings where they gather in His name.
I grab and run, veering toward the movies,
startled hands drop labyrinths,
bags of stony reason,
dogs bark behind their wire fences,
bark, bark, I shout,
the moon is laughing at you,
and so am I.

Depths

Depths, implacable, roam like sharks
through watery greens –
throw them a downy chick,
the soft haunch of a deer,
spring, with all its ribbons flying –
but nothing will appease –
jump onto the sofa,
don't let them bite your ankles
and watch spiders carry webs across the ceiling,
intimacies of the struggle whispered into spider ears –
what are they saying?
"We should have a horse, possibly a spear,
Why is everything so difficult?"
but then, tomorrow comes, fresh as May,
poke its fat side with a stick
and crocuses spill out.

Sparrows fly across my sleep,
a sleep torn and rutted,
its ditches full of sludgy water,
on the floor above, someone sings,
the sound is like a listless breeze
or a bruise fading –
outside spring slides out from under winter
with her blossom legs,
it was kismet, that affair –
soon the peacock sky will travel from the East
stop above our heads –
dusty streets emerge,
jobs will slide around,
the butcher wipe blood stained hands
across his apron,
"and something else?"
consider cows dozing,
their brown slippered hooves
neatly placed beside them,
consider the sun pointing down its muzzle,
while you sit on a park bench
and drink a soda
and watch the blues deepen into waves,
the mind fall, like an orange, into sections –
the clock calls out the hours –
It's got them wrong again, you think
and consider the old dream,
how it twists like a vine through tumbling seasons.

WET FURS

Wet furs,
wheels spinning on thick ice,
buses laden with the day's survivors –
there's the quarry, Miron Fréres on Jarry Street,
summer dust rolled behind its eyes,
its ravings stilled –
there's a snowman in a black fedora
were there stars?
Yes, but I can't remember who they were,
what they said –
Hunger hurried me along,
and my breathe blew out before me
like a little song –
what will you say about the life you had?
A fine snow melted in your hair
in winter time,
the days went by,
you were on the side of idleness,
of doing nothing,
going nowhere,
obsessed with reports the moon was caught again
between bare branches,
miles from town.

Bivouacs

Will things here always be the same?
Bivouacs, late buses,
girls with pepper spray?
It's come to that —
I walked home out of sheer bravado
it was midnight —
a man was peeing in the bushes,
to furtive things I usually shout, HI HO,
but this time kept my counsel —
moved like a soldier toward his tent
along the path laid down by moonlight,
picked my way around broken glass, manifestos,
took a break from longing,
was just a woman walking,
happy, titter tottering.

DAWDLE

We dawdle behind the times,
watch a light weasel out of darkness,
float around a corner of the house –
voices drift through the embroidery of night –
girls we knew,
and their mothers too –
the sun then, spoke Italian,
and the dogs,
and the Pepsi boy, always with his six pack,
his sister buried in the garden as if she were a
    cabbage –
her soul hung like immensity above the street,
wouldn't quite slip through our fingers –
roused by summer, colours brightened,
promise whispered from its throne,
grass grew hot,
pigeons sailed above the churches
skimmed off the prayers
the creamy Sunday vagueness –
parents shimmered like mirages on the far horizon,
the neighbour in a coma slept
and dreamt,
of what?
A white figure in a muffled room,
she was strange music, strangely heard,
the ear, a lonely shell.

Sun cuts the cold into fiery pieces,
they scorch the legs of slow travellers
who never understood the dangers of the road –
hares – there's another slaughtered one –
did anyone hear his whimpers as they hurried by,
did anyone hold him up to their face,
to soothe that loneliness and fear?
One grows tired of sadness,
how it keeps returning,
jumps through splattered windows
or vanishes down streets
that slid out of your journeys
and disappeared East of Queensborough –
I wonder if anyone has lain here
in the middle of this cold month,
pulled a little scarlet willow across their eyes,
smelt the sun,
thought that they could rest here,
half awake, for ever.

One Sits

One sits in a winter coat
and watches brown grass drip,
crows storming through bare branches,
an avalanche of wings,
and recalls stories thumbed through on afternoons
when warmth reeled out of furnaces
glazed fantastic thoughts,
when it was sweet to be in bed at night,
to turn the light out,
to travel up through the roof
and out into creation —
that era vanished around Christmas or the
    Circumcision
the last year of high school,
it left a huge hole in the wall
through which sparrows flew,
their wings mud splattered,
their heads turned to the side
as if prepared for death —
cold, the cold pursued them,
their bones hid beneath their feathers,
except for a leg or two
which stuck out, unceremoniously
and looked useless,
and on the avenues lions were locked inside their
    statues,
and the sky stood back,
when will one know, what one is looking for?

Slow as a snail go the trowel feet
through chaotic rooms
and out onto the porch,
black sounds stir –
where is Daddy's lantern,
a loved one watching from an upper storey window?
Sparrows fidget
but the greedy times have brought no Messiahs –
in the shadows
a story is being slapped together,
vermilion added,
though the end is missing,
and through field grass
go the builders,
what have they constructed
to contain the harrowing night,
to contain the darkness
that rushes toward certain sections of the sky,
certain apartment sides,
huddles with straggly plants,
empty beer cans,
or lingers under bridges
where there are no witnesses,
grows damp and musty,
wraps around the feet?
The trowel feet,
what a miracle, their little steps are.

Now I See

Now I see what we are up against,
disease, diarrhoea,
dull lights, a smelly room,
time,
and too much rouge on sunken cheeks,
it must be fought,
get the pitchfork –
hurry, hurry,
for heat is in its orange sheet,
walls are narrowing,
and we must consult a third party
about these buckling floors,
parrot doors,
about this tying knots with broken threads,
this pulling them apart with eyebrow tweezers,
hurry, hurry, get the hose,
hose me down
while I hoist myself into my favourite hour
and write in my notebook
the things that we are up against.

Bridges

I stand upon bridges,
my arms full of birds
resting from their search for food,
they hop onto my ears, my eyebrows,
my distant destinations –
why are my sides painted black
as if I were a train
stranded between presumption and despair
fighting a dizzy wind,
a lantern in each hand that I swing in circles,
diverging worlds, pulling me apart,
while see saw tunes fly out of violins
on East End corners,
and you weave, my little optimist,
between ginger crowds,
as spring rushes by, her face smeared with heaven.

FISHING

I'm fishing through the drainpipes
for a glittering eye
to plaster over mine,
for a horse to fly above the mysteries –
fishing beneath the smelly scum,
and all about reeds and the hum
of weariness,
and bodies crying in night's riverbed –
don't say a word,
don't console,
you, kissing in your golden bowl.

WEDGED

I'm wedged between odd angles
in my sailor suit,
ships sail around me,
ocean liners.
They know how to navigate,
have radar, and all the latest Morse codes.
Night, in a cashmere coat is lolling on the shore,
they can phone him
get him to wave his arms, release warm breezes –
but something is swimming underwater toward me –
perhaps it is the harbourmaster
chasing minds, unmoored –
are they slipping into secret channels?
I call to them, but hear only seagulls
with their human way of crying.
What is the explanation?
The radio is dead,
the dark has taken over,
has sent its shadows out to get me.
My heart is pounding, my voice rising,
What can I do?
If grandma were alive she'd wring their necks
with her unflinching hands,
fry them up with garlic and with onion –
"save the fat," I hear her now –
oh, where has my champion gone, where has she
      gone?

MUMMIFIES

A coat mummifies the body,
sharp air grows sharper
shaves the bones,
as my head is banged into a door –
they're so clumsy, these porters,
they hurdled me downstairs
and swung me round into the kitchen,
had their coffee, toast, their rock and roll –
my valuables were left behind,
my black eye shadow, my harmonica,
good bye, good luck, no one said it,
so I drew a circle round myself
to keep the cold winds out,
decided not to send out cards
with my new address.
Once there, I'll snuggle down,
keep my snout close to the ground
knowing they'll come in a soft series,
chilly and ripe,
mango days.

So now it's raining
and we've arranged our shaky legs
one atop another
and thrown all the kitchen knives,
maimed the worldly hero,
rendered him incapable of movement –
let's carry him to bed,
stuff his glamour in the dirty nylons drawer,
put his leather in the compost heap –
we'll read him best sellers,
feed him taco chips –
won't grandma be pleased, there in her floured apron
with her apple strudel, the best in town,
perhaps the parish priest will bless us,
leave a holy candle,
which we'll slip underneath the linens
with the bank book
and life's unusual contraptions,
and we'll feel free to love the cobwebs
on the kitchen ceiling,
to hide behind the door and contemplate our journeys,
to stand with snails beneath dripping eaves
out on our own veranda.

B ED

I lie in bed above a boggy floor
of nothingness,
a glass of gingerale bubbling in one hand,
read Italian poets.
It's a hard life,
sneaking through the evening
while vermilion drips drops of red
onto stony streets –
silent, everything is silent
except for reckless sirens racing,
as if toward the center of the universe –
they scream past sleeping rain,
past the berry bushes –
"Not now, I'm reading,"
I plead – too late,
they woke the prowler in the basement –
he pulls on cougar stockings with velvet soles,
smacks the furnace with a ski pole,
his signal for the circus to begin.
Will you express yourself more clearly,
I shout into the waiting stillness –
No answer, answers –
Does he even know my maiden name,
or that I've filled my pockets with the twittering of
        birds,
that I have my own responses?

FEET

We washed our feet on Fridays –
sat before the fire
with our tub of soapy water –
night, in a circle round the house
closing in and rushing back –
squirrels caught in the middle,
hazel nuts,
scraps of mild weather.
Snow crept across the backs of dogs, hedges,
climbed the North wall.
The moon peered in the window
saw us, each with a leg extended in mid air,
examining our calves, ankles, toes,
our happiness,
that still is there, unmoved by circumstance –
still is writing above the years
its story without a plot, without a hero,
without an end.